D1450233

TOYS

THROUGH TIME

TOYS
THROUGH
TIME

Chris Oxlade

RSVP
RAINTREE
STECK-VAUGHN
P U B L I S H E R S
The Steck-Vaughn Company

Austin, Texas

Published by Raintree Steck-Vaughn Publishers,
an imprint of Steck-Vaughn Company

Macdonald Young Books
Design and Typesetting: Roger Kohn Designs
Illustration: Coral Mula, Ross Watton
Commissioning Editor: Debbie Fox
Editor: Caroline Wilson
Picture Research: Val Mulcahy
Consultant: Paul Atterbury

Raintree Steck-Vaughn Publishers staff
Editor: Kathy DeVico
Project Manager: Joyce Spicer

Photo Acknowledgments
We are grateful to the following for permission to
reproduce photographs: Antikenmuseum/Staatliche Museen
Preubischer Kulturbestiz, Berlin (photo: Johannes Laurentius),
p.8; The Bodleian Library, Oxford MS. Douce 8, p.6, p.12; Clive
Corless, p.14, p.22; Paul Mulcahy, p.36; The National Trust
Photographic Library, p.18; Robert Opie, p.28; Sotheby's, p.32;
Vtech Electronics (UK) plc, p.40

The publishers would like to thank the following for their help:
Clive Corless; LEGO U.K. Limited; Mark Mulcahy; Helen Nolan;
Sony Computer Entertainment Europe.

Library of Congress Cataloging-in-Publication Data

Oxlade, Chris.
    Toys / Chris Oxlade.
        p. cm. — (Through time)
    Includes index.
    ISBN 0–8172–4139–6
    1. Toys — History — Juvenile literature.
    2. Toy making — Juvenile literature.
    3. Toys — Design and construction — Juvenile literature.
    [1. Toys — History. 2. Toy making.]
    I. Title II. Series.
    GV1218.5.094 1996
    790. 1' 33 — dc20   95–23173
                         CIP
                         AC

Printed and bound in Hong Kong.
1 2 3 4 5 6 7 8 9 0 99 98 97 96 95

CONTENTS

THE FIRST TOYS

The earliest toys we know of were made over two thousand years ago in Ancient Egypt. Archaeologists have found toys such as balls, tops, and dolls in Egyptian tombs. The toys were intended to be for the dead person to play with in the next world, where the Egyptians believed their souls went when they died. Pictures of children playing with wheeled toys also appear in Egyptian wall paintings. The toys were all homemade from simple materials like clay, wood, and reeds from the banks of the Nile River. Children in Ancient Greece and Rome played with a wider range of toys than Egyptian children, including hobbyhorses and toy soldiers. Some were more complex in construction than Egyptian toys, but they were still made from everyday materials.

Many ancient types of toys are still popular today. This detail from a vase from Ancient Greece shows a boy playing with a yo-yo.

A WOODEN TOY TIGER
This toy tiger was found in the ruins of the Ancient Egyptian city of Thebes. It was probably made around 1000 B.C. It has glass eyes, bronze teeth, and a jaw worked by a string.

MAKE A PULL-ALONG TOY

1. Make an animal from modeling clay. Mold the head, tail, and legs from small lumps of clay before attaching them to the body.

2. Push holes for axles with a piece of wooden dowel or a pencil. Use two pieces of dowel or drinking straws for axles.

3. Add four clay wheels and a string to pull the toy along.

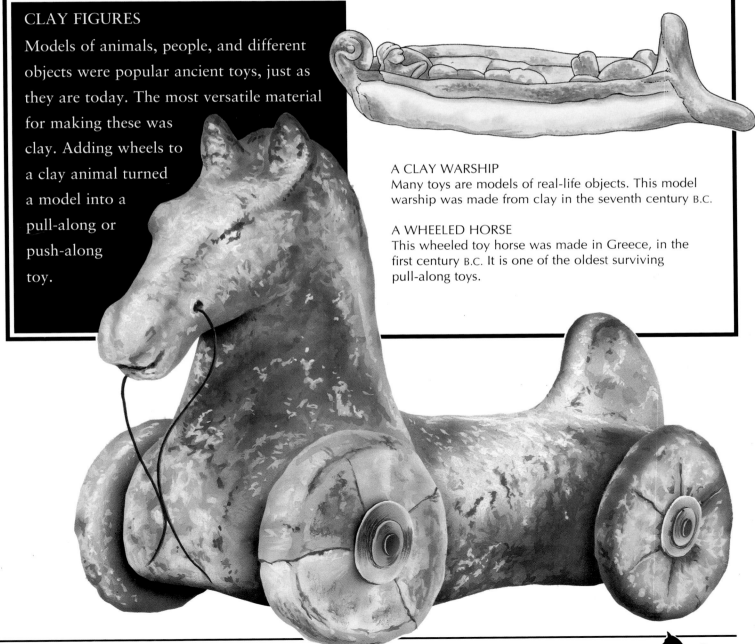

CLAY FIGURES

Models of animals, people, and different objects were popular ancient toys, just as they are today. The most versatile material for making these was clay. Adding wheels to a clay animal turned a model into a pull-along or push-along toy.

A CLAY WARSHIP
Many toys are models of real-life objects. This model warship was made from clay in the seventh century B.C.

A WHEELED HORSE
This wheeled toy horse was made in Greece, in the first century B.C. It is one of the oldest surviving pull-along toys.

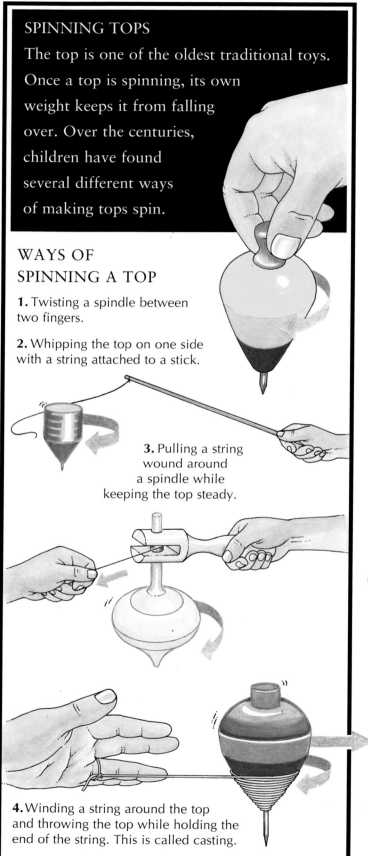

SPINNING TOPS

The top is one of the oldest traditional toys. Once a top is spinning, its own weight keeps it from falling over. Over the centuries, children have found several different ways of making tops spin.

WAYS OF SPINNING A TOP

1. Twisting a spindle between two fingers.

2. Whipping the top on one side with a string attached to a stick.

3. Pulling a string wound around a spindle while keeping the top steady.

4. Winding a string around the top and throwing the top while holding the end of the string. This is called casting.

SIMPLE TOYS OF TODAY

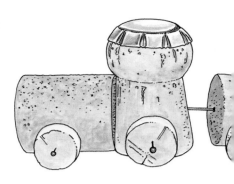

A toy train made from corks, pins, and wire.

Children still make their own simple toys, just as they did before there were toys to buy. They use simple materials, such as clay or wood, or even pieces of trash. The toys that children in one country make are often similar to those made by children in other countries. They are traditional toys, such as rag dolls or spinning tops, or models of everyday objects, like telephones or cars. Toys like these can be highly decorated, with paints and colored paper, fabric and yarn, or they can be left quite plain.

This modern whip top from Bulgaria looks as if it could have been played with in the Middle Ages. In fact, the design has not changed for hundreds of years.

THE DEVELOPMENT OF TOPS

Simple tops have changed very little for hundreds of years, but there have been some innovations.

AROUND 2000 B.C. A clay spinning top from Ancient Egypt.

Small, simple toys, such as plastic figures, are often as much fun to play with as larger, more complicated toys. Small plastic toy parts can be made quickly and automatically by machines. This mass production means that they are cheap to make and, therefore, cheap to buy. When you play with simple toys, you have to use your own imagination, just as children did thousands of years ago. In addition to making them move, you can make up stories and adventures for them.

Plastic doll models of characters from films and television programs are very popular toys today. They normally have a few movable or interchangeable parts.

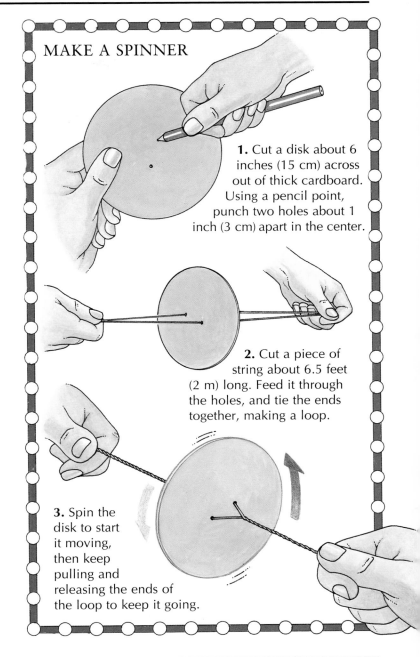

MAKE A SPINNER

1. Cut a disk about 6 inches (15 cm) across out of thick cardboard. Using a pencil point, punch two holes about 1 inch (3 cm) apart in the center.

2. Cut a piece of string about 6.5 feet (2 m) long. Feed it through the holes, and tie the ends together, making a loop.

3. Spin the disk to start it moving, then keep pulling and releasing the ends of the loop to keep it going.

MIDDLE AGES
A picture from a medieval manuscript. It shows a child playing with a double-tailed whip top.

1950s
A tinplate plunger top, which is spun by moving the spiral plunger up and down.

1970s
A gyroscope with a frame that stays still as the inner flywheel turns. The same principle is used in compasses for navigation.

quindeam annis

TOY PINWHEELS
This picture is part of a sixteenth-century manuscript. The child is playing with a pinwheel.

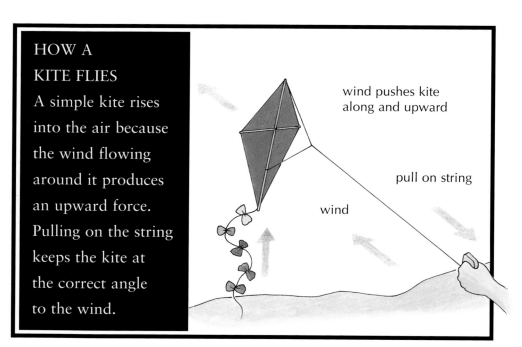

The Roman Empire came to an end in the fifth century A.D. Historians call the five hundred years that followed the Dark Ages, because Europe fell into chaos. There were frequent wars, and some skills and types of craftsmanship were lost or forgotten. Children had to make do with a few simple toys, such as rag dolls. After the Dark Ages, toy-making skills began to reappear.

HOW A KITE FLIES
A simple kite rises into the air because the wind flowing around it produces an upward force. Pulling on the string keeps the kite at the correct angle to the wind.

wind pushes kite along and upward

pull on string

wind

A JAPANESE FIGURE KITE
A traditional Japanese figure kite from the nineteenth century. Kites were popular toys in Japan and China, because paper and bamboo were cheap materials.

Craftsmen once again made toys to sell at markets and fairs. In addition to the toys of the Romans, children also had new types of toys, including some that were powered by the wind, such as toy windmills and kites. In fact, kites were invented in China, probably as early as 200 B.C. Kite-making ideas reached Europe in the late fourteenth century.

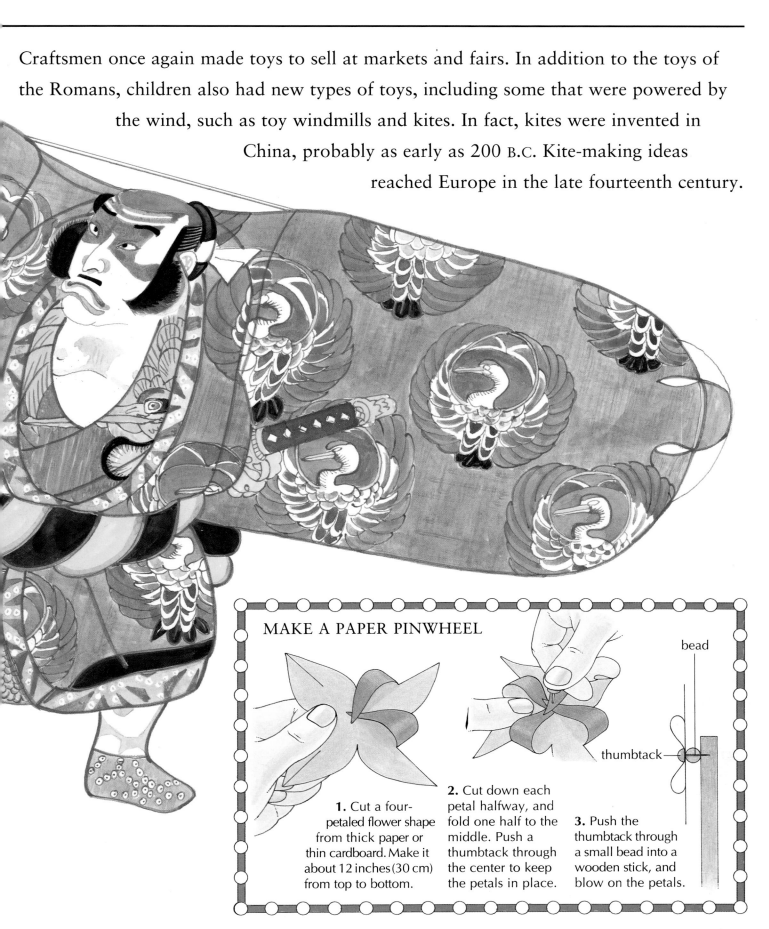

MAKE A PAPER PINWHEEL

1. Cut a four-petaled flower shape from thick paper or thin cardboard. Make it about 12 inches (30 cm) from top to bottom.

2. Cut down each petal halfway, and fold one half to the middle. Push a thumbtack through the center to keep the petals in place.

bead

thumbtack

3. Push the thumbtack through a small bead into a wooden stick, and blow on the petals.

TOYS FOR EVERYONE

FLAT MODEL SOLDIERS
Three flat model soldiers — a standard-bearer and two foot soldiers. They are about 2 inches (5 cm) high and ⅛ inch (3 mm) thick.

From the fourteenth century onward, European merchants began to trade more and more widely. Craftsmen began to manufacture things, including toys, in large numbers for export abroad. But most manufactured toys were still too expensive for ordinary people to buy. Dollhouses and other luxuries were only available to wealthy children.

By the eighteenth century, manufacturers were beginning to make toys from a variety of materials. Most were still made from wood, but soldiers and other figures were being cast in metals, such as tin, lead, and pewter. Other new toy-making materials were paper, papier-mâché, china, and tinplate. Tinplate is a thin sheet of steel covered in a very thin coat of tin. As manufacturing methods improved, toys became cheaper to buy.

A PEWTER MONKEY
Pewter is an alloy (mixture) of tin and small amounts of other metals. Pewter was a common material. It was used for plates and cups, until china and porcelain replaced it in the eighteenth century.

A LEAD FLAT KNIGHT
The first metal toy soldiers were called flats, because they were flat models with detail on one or both sides.

HOW A FLAT WAS MADE

1. The contours of the model were carved in reverse into two slate blocks. The blocks were placed tightly together to make a hollow mold.

2. Molten tin was poured through a small hole in the top of the mold.

3. When the tin had cooled and turned solid, the mold was opened. The model was then welded to a tin base.

HOW A TINPLATE MODEL WAS MADE

1. The colored decoration for both sides of the model was printed onto a flat sheet of tinplate.

2. The pieces were cut out and pressed into shapes by machine.

3. The pieces were joined together. This was done by bending small tabs on one piece around the edges of the next piece.

PRESSED TINPLATE HORSE AND CARRIAGE

The earliest pressed tinplate toys were cut from plain metal. But soon the tinplate sheets were being printed with details before the pieces were pressed out. Tinplate toys are still being made.

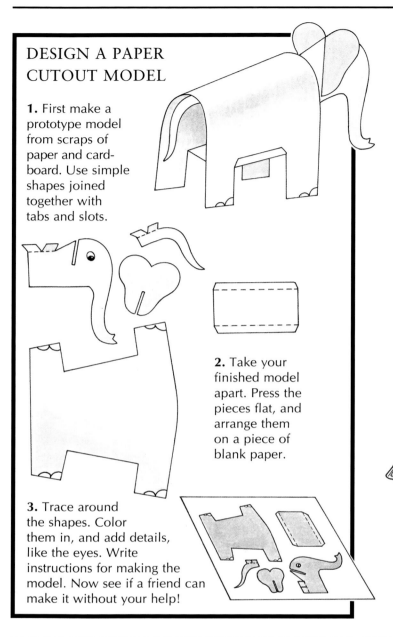

DESIGN A PAPER CUTOUT MODEL

1. First make a prototype model from scraps of paper and cardboard. Use simple shapes joined together with tabs and slots.

2. Take your finished model apart. Press the pieces flat, and arrange them on a piece of blank paper.

3. Trace around the shapes. Color them in, and add details, like the eyes. Write instructions for making the model. Now see if a friend can make it without your help!

PAPER TOYS

In the eighteenth and nineteenth centuries, paper was widely used in toy-making. The most common paper toys were cutout sheets. Printed shapes were sold in sheets. Children could stick these onto cardboard, cut them out, and join them together to make a finished toy. Theaters complete with scenery and actors, ships, and dolls supplied with a change of paper clothes were all popular types of cutout sheet toys. Papier-mâché was also used for making figures, and especially for molding dolls' heads.

A PAPER DOLL
Paper dolls often came with dresses, wigs, and hats — all in the latest fashions.

MATERIALS THROUGH THE AGES

Many different materials have been used for making toys. Here are a few of the most important ones.

ANCIENT EGYPTIAN TIMES TO TODAY
Clay, along with wood, was one of the first toy-making materials. Modeling clay is still popular.

SEVENTEENTH TO NINETEENTH CENTURIES
A wax coating gave a doll's head and arms a lifelike appearance.

A MODERN STUFFED TOY

Quality stuffed toys have a label showing that they have been made to a strict standard.

DANGER AND SAFETY

Until the second half of the twentieth century, toys were made without much thought for children's safety. By today's standards, many of them would seem quite dangerous. In many countries, there are now strict safety rules that toy manufacturers must follow by law. Stuffed toys, such as teddy bears, must not be made or stuffed with flammable materials that could burst into flames if the toy were too close to a fire. Toys for very young children must not have tiny pieces that a child could pull off and possibly swallow. Substances that we know are poisonous, like lead, are no longer allowed to be used in toy-making.

1840s TO 1930s
Rubber was molded into dolls' heads, animals, and squeaking toys. Then early plastics, like celluloid, were used.

1950s TO TODAY
Plastic is now the main toy-making material. There is more about plastic on pages 36–38.

TEDDY BEARS

Toy bears had been popular for a hundred years before teddy bears appeared. They were much more realistic and stood on all fours. The first teddy bear was made in the United States in 1903. The design was based on a bear from a cartoon about President Roosevelt, whose nickname was Teddy. Bears subsequently became more furry, and some were made with extra features, like squeaks and growls.

This is one of the oldest teddy bears still in existence. It was made in 1907, from burlap and cotton, and was stuffed with sawdust.

DOLLS

Lady Arabella Stuart, a cousin of Elizabeth I of England, holding a doll in Elizabethan clothes. Although the little girl is only 23 months old, it is interesting that her doll is a replica of a lady, and not of a baby or child, like the dolls played with by today's toddlers.

From Ancient Egyptian times to the present day, dolls have been one of the most popular toys of all. In fact, dolls were among the very first toys, although we do not know when the first doll was made. Archaeologists have found ancient figures made of clay or wood that may have been ornaments, religious statues, or dolls to play with. Greek and Roman dolls had bodies made from wood or clay, sometimes with jointed limbs. Toy manufacturers began to make dolls in large numbers in the eighteenth century. They tried many different materials for making dolls' heads. Wood, wax, papier-mâché, and various ceramics were all used successfully. Soon, novel dolls with closing eyes, baby dolls that drank from a bottle, and talking dolls began to appear.

TYPES OF HEADS

Doll manufacturers tried many materials to make heads that would be realistic, durable, and cheap to make. Two of the best materials were wax, which was used as an outer coating, and bisque, a type of porcelain.

Wax head   Bisque head

The parts of a doll's body that were hidden under its clothes were normally made with cheaper materials than the head and shoulders, and the lower arms and legs.

Wooden jointed body with porcelain head and shoulders, forearms, and lower legs.

Stuffed cloth body with porcelain head, shoulders, forearms, and lower legs.

Complete porcelain or composition body for a doll sold without clothes.

A German doll with a bisque head, made in the late nineteenth century. It has glass eyes and a wig made from mohair.

MODERN DOLLS

FASHION DOLLS
Many different outfits are available for modern dolls, including a wide variety of shoes, jewelry, and other fashion accessories.

RAG DOLLS
Dolls do not necessarily need to look realistic. Rag dolls can be just as much fun to play with.

DOLLS THROUGH THE AGES
The main changes in dolls through the ages have been in the materials used to make them.

Today, you can buy hundreds of different types of dolls. Most of them are mass-produced in plastic, which makes a basic doll cheap to buy. Wooden and rag dolls are also available, but they have to be made by hand and are often more expensive than plastic dolls. Modern dolls can be very simple or very complicated. Some are made from just one or two pieces of colored plastic, with no movable limbs. Others have movable arms and legs, real clothes, and hair that can be styled. Some of the latest dolls even contain electronics and other gadgets that make them talk, cry, and wet their diapers. One of the most famous dolls to appear in recent times is Barbie®. In addition to the basic doll, you can buy outfits for every occasion, makeup, cars, houses, and even boyfriends!

200 B.C.
The Romans made some of the first jointed dolls. This one has real gold bracelets.

EIGHTEENTH CENTURY
Small wooden dolls, called Dutch dolls, were popular for dollhouses.

MAKING A DOLL WITH JOINTED LIMBS

1. Join together the outer sleeves from two empty matchboxes end-to-end with tape.

2. Cut two arms, two upper legs, and two lower legs out of stiff cardboard. Using a sharp pencil, punch holes in the body, legs, and arms where the joints will be.

3. Assemble the legs, and attach the limbs by threading string through the holes and tying the ends.

4. Paint a face on the doll, and stick on hair made from short pieces of string. Make some clothes as well, if you like.

1878
The first talking doll was made by the American inventor, Thomas Edison. The sound was made by a phonograph, which was the first successful sound-recording machine.

1990s
A modern doll made of synthetic materials, such as plastic. She has Rollerblades®, sunglasses, and earrings.

TOYS THAT MOVE

Mechanical toys with moving parts, such as walking dolls, animated pictures, and performing acrobats, became very popular in the eighteenth and nineteenth centuries. There were hundreds of different types of mechanical toys. Some were simple, like the balancing toys shown here. Some were more complex, with clockwork power, such as a model man who repeatedly raised a cigar to his mouth. Most expensive were very detailed models of people who performed complicated feats, such as card tricks. These were called automata (see pages 26 – 27) and were really toys meant for adults!

JACK-IN-THE-BOX
An American jack-in-the-box from the 1950s. It is also a windup, tin-made musical box.

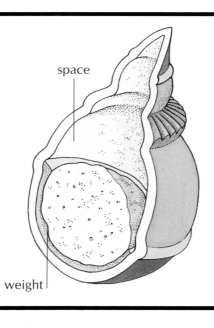

This swaying figure has counterweights that keep it balanced on its thin stand.

Balancing dolls with heavily weighted bases like this weeble-type doll are found all over the world.

HOW A BALANCING DOLL WORKS

A balancing doll has a lightweight, hollow body and a round, heavy base. If the doll tips to one side, the weight becomes off-center and pulls the doll upright again.

space

weight

An automaton, called the Dancing Punchinello. Winding the handle makes the figure dance, while music plays in the box.

MAKE A TIGHTROPE WALKER

Counterweight balancing toys balance because most of the weight of the figure is lower than the point on which the figure rests. You can see how this works for yourself by making this balancing tightrope walker.

1. Draw a figure on stiff cardboard, color it, and cut it out.

2. Cut a V-shaped slot in the bottom of one of the figure's feet.

3. Bend a piece of thin wire into a curve, and attach it to the back of the figure's hands with putty.

4. Add blobs of putty to the ends of the wire to make the figure balance on a tight string.

ACROBATS

A typical acrobat toy. The hands are attached to the pole, which is moved by hand to make the figure somersault.

The legs are jointed so that they swing freely.

Simple moving toys had to be operated by twisting a knob or pulling a string. Some very common examples were acrobats that swung around a horizontal bar; hammer toys, where two figures hit an anvil alternately; and a monkey on a stick that worked in a similar way to the swinging acrobat.

PECKING BIRDS

Another type of mechanical toy was operated by a swinging weight. These toys appeared in the second half of the nineteenth century. You held the toy by its handle, and moved it to and fro or around and around to keep the weight swinging. As the weight moved, it pulled on different strings in turn, making different parts of the toy move. Swinging weight toys often showed scenes that included people and animals. A well-known example is the pecking birds toy. As the weight swings, the birds peck the ground in turn, making a tapping noise.

NEW IDEAS FOR MOVING TOYS

Here are a few moving toys that have appeared in the twentieth century. As technology has advanced, and more modern materials have become available, people have been able to make many other simple toys whose appeal for children lies in the way they move.

1950s
This toy's limbs, neck, and tail are kept rigid with elastic strings inside. Pressing a button under the base makes it collapse comically.

THE PANTIN

The pantin was one of the most popular toys ever. It was a figure, such as a clown or dancer, with legs and arms that could rotate at the hips and shoulders. Pulling the strings at the top and bottom made the arms and legs rise upward. The first pantins were made as children's toys, but they soon became trendy as an entertainment for adults.

MAKE A PANTIN

1. Cut a body shape without arms and legs out of stiff cardboard.

2. Cut two arms and two legs from the same cardboard.

3. Poke holes in the body and limbs, and join them together with paper fasteners.

3. Attach strings to the legs and arms. Join them as shown, and add another string to the top.

1960s
The Slinky® is a steel or colored plastic spring that moves down a staircase on its own.

1970s
Sticky rubber feet keep this window-walking toy attached to the glass as it tumbles downward.

1980s
Inside this car is a tiny flywheel-powered motor that is wound up by dragging the car across the floor. The car then shoots forward for a few seconds. This mechanism was invented in the 1940s.

HISTORY OF AUTOMATA

Mechanical figures and animals have been made for thousands of years. They were most popular during the eighteenth century. Today, there are very few toys that you simply wind up and watch, except for some aimed at tiny children.

SECOND CENTURY B.C.
A steam-driven automaton built by the Greek scientist, Hero of Alexandria.

HOW AUTOMATA WORK

Automata were powered by clockwork. Winding them up normally turned a shaft that caused the model to move. Different methods were developed to make the shaft work other movements, such as the up and down movement of an arm.

SIMPLE AUTOMATA MECHANISMS

1. A shaped wheel, called a cam, makes the rod rise slowly and then fall, four times for each turn of the shaft.

2. A string attached to a peg on a wheel is pulled up and down, once for every turn of the shaft.

AUTOMATA

Automata are moving toys that perform clever feats and actions entirely by themselves. Simple automata were made in medieval times, but their real rise in popularity came during the eighteenth century. Automata were normally built by watchmakers and clockmakers to show off their skills. The most complicated examples took years to design and make. They were toys for grown-ups to show off to their friends rather than for children to play with, and were seen as fascinating curiosities — museum pieces in their own era.

THE WRITER
This mechanical figure writes on paper, and its eyes watch the pen as it moves. The figure was made in the 1770s.

THIRTEENTH
CENTURY ONWARD
Automatic figures were
built to strike the hours on
the front of decorative
church clocks.

1950s
Battery-powered walking
robots were made popular
by the interest in science
fiction and space travel.

1980s
This electronic vehicle can be programmed
to carry out movements
automatically.

One of the most famous automata makers was
a Frenchman, Jacques de Vaucanson. He made
many automata that were exhibited all over
Europe, where they amazed the people who
flocked to see them. They included a flute player
that played twelve tunes, and a duck that swam,
drank water, and even ate and digested food!
Not all automata were so advanced. Simpler
ones were mass-produced, mostly made of
tinplate and with clockwork mechanisms. Some
even used the working principle of an egg-timer,
being powered by falling sand. Many automata
were models of figures that played
musical instruments, lovingly
reproduced in miniature.

MOVING PICTURES

Moving picture toys were a combination
of a picture in a frame and an automatic toy.

1. A sand-powered toy.
Falling sand turns a
hidden wheel, making
the monkey's arm move.
Turning the box upside
down for a few seconds,
then the right way up,
sets the toy going again.

CLOCKWORK OARSMAN
This mechanical oarsman rows his
boat across the water, like a real-life rower.
The toy was made in the United States, in 1869.

2. Other
sources of
power were
clockwork, and even
steam. Here, steam makes
the cat play the violin and the
kittens dance.

OPTICAL TOYS

In nineteenth-century Europe, people became fascinated by toys that created some sort of magic optical effect, or illusion. These included toys that made photographs or paintings appear three-dimensional, toys that produced recognizable pictures from strange patterns, and toys that produced moving pictures.

One reason that these toys were so popular in the early nineteenth century was that the first successful photographs were now being taken. The interest in toys and other machines that could produce moving pictures led inventors to develop the idea of the movie.

A VICTORIAN FILOSCOPE
The filoscope was an early kind of flick book. On each page was a frame from a moving picture. Flicking through the book rapidly made the picture seem to move.

PANORAMA TOYS
Panorama toys showed pictures of famous events in a new and unusual way. One type consisted of a series of cutout scenes, set one behind the other, inside an accordion-like tube. When you looked through a hole at one end, the receding frames gave an exciting impression of depth in the picture.

Long, narrow spaces, such as the insides of cathedrals and tunnels, made good panoramas.

THE THAUMATROPE

The thaumatrope was one of the earliest and simplest optical toys. Spinning the disk quickly made the two pictures on the opposite sides appear to combine into one picture.

THE ZOETROPE

The zoetrope appeared in the 1860s. It consisted of an open revolving drum with narrow slits around the top. A strip of pictures, each slightly different than the one before, was placed inside the drum. You spun the drum and looked into it through the slits. As each slit passed your eye, you caught a glimpse of the picture on the opposite side of the drum. The sequence of pictures created the illusion of movement. Picture sequence disks could also be put in the base for added effect. The phenakistoscope was a flat disk with slits around the edge that worked in a similar way as the zoetrope.

MAKE A THAUMATROPE

1. On a piece of paper, draw a circle about 4 inches (10 cm) across with the complete picture on it (for example, a jockey on a horse). Mark positions for the two holes for the strings, one at each side.

2. Trace the circle, the hole positions, and one part of the picture (for example, the horse). Stick the tracing on a piece of cardboard, and cut out the circle.

3. Trace the circle again, with the hole positions and the other part of the picture (for example, the jockey). Cut out the second circle of tracing paper, and stick it upside down on the other side of the cardboard circle. Make sure that the hole positions on each side match up.

4. Poke the two holes, and tie a piece of string through each. Twist the strings in your fingers to make the thaumatrope work.

MOVING PICTURE MACHINES

Moving images, such as films and television pictures, are not really moving at all. They are made up of still pictures, called frames, which we see one after the other in quick succession. Our eyes cannot react fast enough to see each individual frame, so we see a moving image instead.

The oldest and simplest moving picture toy is the flick book. This is a small

book with a frame from a moving picture on each page. Looking at the pages while quickly flicking through the book creates the moving picture. Modern moving picture toys and games work electronically. Some of these display pictures on a television or a similar sort of screen, where

A sequence from a zoetrope. Each frame is slightly different from the one before.

Activating sections of an LCD (liquid crystal display) screen, one after the other, gives the impression that an object is moving.

MAKE A PHENAKISTOSCOPE

1. Cut a circle out of cardboard about 10 inches (25 cm) across. Using a pencil and ruler, divide the circle into eight equal segments.

2. Cut a slot 2 inches (5 cm) long and 1 cm wide at the end of each pencil line.

3. Draw a moving picture with eight frames. Cut out the frames, and stick one at the bottom of each slot. The top of each frame must be nearest the slot.

4. Push a pencil through the middle of the circle. Stand in front of a mirror, and spin the disk. Look through the slots to see the moving picture in the mirror.

DEVELOPMENTS IN OPTICAL TOYS

With their brass cases and glass lenses, the first optical toys looked more like scientific instruments than toys. Plastic lenses made them cheaper and stronger.

each frame is shown for a split second. Simple toys, like the one shown here, have a screen like an electronic watch. There are shapes in set positions on the screen. Making these shapes appear and disappear in the correct order creates the illusion that they are moving.

You can find out more about electronic toys on pages 40-43.

HOW A 3-D PICTURE TOY WORKS

Three-dimensional picture toys actually display two pictures, one for each of the viewer's eyes. The pictures show a scene viewed from two slightly different places, which is how our eyes actually see a scene. Our brains are fooled into seeing a picture with depth and solid objects, rather than a flat picture.

Pairs of pictures for 3-D viewing are called stereo pictures. Try viewing this example. Put your index finger on the page between the two pictures, and then gradually lift it. Keep looking at your finger, and the two pictures will merge together.

EARLY NINETEENTH CENTURY
The kaleidoscope produces a pattern by reflecting colored pieces of glass in two mirrors.

1860s TO 1930s
The magic lantern projects a picture from a slide onto a screen. The light is provided by a kerosene lamp.

1960s
This View Master® has interchangeable story disks. Rotating the disk shows the next picture in the story.

1980s TO TODAY
Cheap pocket electronic games have small liquid crystal displays, similar to those in electronic watches.

TRANSPORTATION AND POWER

Many types of toys are models of real-life things, and some of the most common are toy vehicles. They became popular as new forms of transportation, such as trains and cars, were developed during the nineteenth century. Toy manufacturers brought out toy versions of machines very soon after the real things had appeared. The first transportation toys had to be pushed or pulled along. But before long, methods of powering the toys, such as clockwork and friction, were invented. Some toys used the same sort of engine as the real thing, only in miniature form. Just as today, some transportation toys were cheap and simple, while others were more accurate models, and thus more expensive.

TINPLATE TOYS
Three tinplate toy cars. Two were made in Germany in the 1930s, and the other was made in Japan in 1958.

MAKE A POWERED VEHICLE

1. Stretch two rubber bands around the rims of a spool of thread.

2. Using a hacksaw, cut a slice of candle about ¼ inch (5 mm) thick. Make a hole in the middle with a ¼ inch (5 mm) drill bit held in your fingers. Thread a rubber band through the spool of thread and candle slice. Put a piece of dowel through the candle end, and a paper clip through the other.

3. Attach the paper clip to the spool of thread with two thumbtacks.

4. Wind the dowel around and around, put the vehicle on a flat surface, and let it go. NOTE: Ask an adult to help you use the hacksaw and the drill bit.

candle

paper clip

dowel

rubber band

thumbtacks

TOY TRAINS

The first toy trains were based on the first real trains of the early nineteenth century, such as the famous Stephenson's Rocket.

Not all toy trains run on tracks. This simple American tinplate carpet train was made in the 1870s.

A PADDLE STEAMER and LIGHTHOUSE

These tinplate toys were made by Märklin, a famous German toy manufacturer. Tinplate models were strong and durable, but many tinplate toy boats were lost when they sank in ponds!

As technology has advanced, new forms of remote control for toys have been developed.

1950s
The rotor of this helicopter is turned by a handle on a remote control. These helicopters flew rather erratically.

1960s
The electric motor in this truck is switched on and reversed with the remote control, which also carries the steering control.

ELECTRIC POWER

Today, electricity is the most common form of power for remote-controlled toys. The electric energy is stored in a battery, or comes from the electric power source. An electric motor changes the electric energy into movement. The first electric toys were toy trains made in the 1890s. They ran on batteries that only produced a weak electric current, and their motors were too large for small models. Small, reliable, electric motors were not developed until the 1930s. By the 1960s, many moving toys had electric motors powered by batteries.

TRACK POWER

Modern toy locomotives are controlled by remote control. A transformer can change the amount of electricity in the rails, and thus vary the speed of the train.

A paper cutout model airplane from 1909.

MODEL AIRPLANES

The first toy airplanes appeared at the beginning of the twentieth century, soon after the first real airplane flights. The first toy airplane that could actually fly was made in 1907.

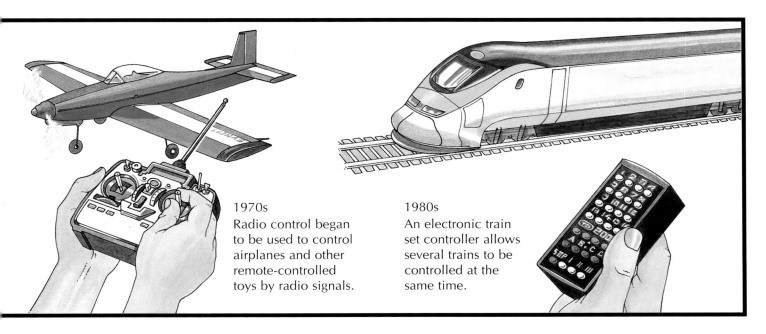

1970s
Radio control began to be used to control airplanes and other remote-controlled toys by radio signals.

1980s
An electronic train set controller allows several trains to be controlled at the same time.

CONSTRUCTION SYSTEMS

Modern toy construction sets allow children to build different types of vehicles, all by themselves. The parts can be put together with a special power wrench. Some kits even come with a battery powered motor.

A motorcycle, complete with shock absorbers and handlebars.

CLOCKWORK

A WINDUP CROCODILE
This bathtub toy has a clockwork-powered wagging tail.

Clockwork is a cheap and simple form of power. Until the 1960s, most remote-controlled toys were moved by clockwork, and it is still used for some cheap toys. A clockwork toy does not need new batteries every few weeks and can be played with in water, whereas an electric toy would be ruined. Its disadvantages are that the speed of a clockwork motor cannot be controlled very well, and it needs regular winding.

PLASTIC TOYS

The greatest change ever in toy manufacturing came during the 1950s. This was the time when plastics became widely available. Plastics can be molded and shaped when they are hot, and become solid when they cool down. Before plastic, an artificial material, called celluloid, was patented in 1870 and used for toy parts for a long time. But it could catch fire quickly and was too easily broken for toys that might get rough treatment. Scientists began to understand plastics better in the 1920s, and new plastics began to appear. Manufacturing techniques, such as vacuum molding, were developed. This allowed plastics to be made into complex shapes. The process of manufacturing plastic items is easily automated, and by the 1950s, plastic toys were being made cheaply and in the millions.

VACUUM CLEANER TOY
Modern plastics can be made in almost any color. So bright, colorful toys can be produced without painting them.

A LEGO® set that shows the range of shapes that can be made from plastic. With a little imagination, you can build almost anything from LEGO® sets.

USING PLASTIC

There are many different types of plastic, and each one has its own characteristics that make it good for certain jobs.

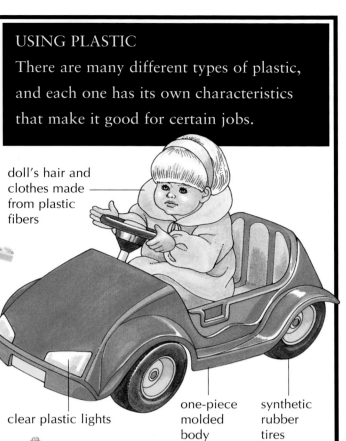

doll's hair and clothes made from plastic fibers

clear plastic lights

one-piece molded body

synthetic rubber tires

HOW A VACUUM MOLD WORKS

1. Find a small plastic bottle. Unscrew the top. Ask an adult to help you punch several holes in the base.

2. Build a shape, such as a face, with modeling clay on the bottom of the bottle. Make sure you leave some of the holes uncovered.

3. Cut the neck off a balloon, and stretch it over the shape.

4. Suck the air out of the bottle through the neck. The balloon should mold itself to the shape.

1935
Nylon was first produced as a fiber for textile-making. In toy-making it is used for small gearwheels and propellers.

NEW MATERIALS

Exciting new materials with new properties are being developed all the time. Here are some that are widely used for toys.

1940
Polyethylene is a soft plastic that can be molded into complicated shapes.

1943
Polyvinyl chloride (PVC) can be made into sheets, as used in this playhouse, or molded into shapes.

PLASTIC CONSTRUCTION KITS

The parts of a plastic construction kit come joined together because they are made in one piece in a mold.

paint, brush, and glue

decals

plastic pieces

OUTDOOR TOYS

Plastics are waterproof and durable, making them ideal for outdoor toys.

HOPPER
This inflatable toy is made from synthetic rubber, which can stretch and return to shape without being damaged.

A CHANGE OF MATERIALS

During the 1950s and 1960s, plastics almost completely replaced other toy-making materials. They replaced tinplate for making toys, because molded plastic parts could be given much more realistic detail than tinplate parts, and could be glued or made to snap together. Dolls were made completely from flesh-colored plastic. These were much more durable and realistic than the china-headed dolls. Wooden seats on outdoor toys, like swings, were replaced with plastic ones. Small toys, such as dollhouse cups and plates, became much cheaper because they could now be manufactured in plastic in large numbers. Plastic is now the most commonly used toy-making material, but it is not suitable for every job. Metal is used where extra strength is needed, and many beautiful wooden toys are still made for younger children.

TOY SOLDIERS
Early toy soldiers (left) were made, one at a time, from metal or wood. Using plastic, small pieces like soldiers can now be made hundreds at a time. Plastic-based paints make them easy to decorate (above).

PEDAL VEHICLES
Plastic can be combined with other weatherproof materials, like metals, to make pedal-powered vehicles.

SLIDES
Modern plastics, like PVC, can be molded into large shapes, like the parts of this slide.

SPACE-AGE TOYS

Electronic educational toys can help children as young as four years old learn spelling or arithmetic in a fun way. The machines can speak their questions and answers.

Electronics and computers have had an enormous effect on toy-making, just as they have in many other areas of our lives. The first breakthrough in electronics was the development of the transistor (a type of electronic switch), in 1948. Then, in 1958, the first silicon chip was made. This allowed large numbers of electronic components, such as transistors and resistors, to fit into a tiny space. Previously, they had been very bulky and expensive. No one even considered using them in toys. Gradually electronic components and silicon chips became cheaper and easier to produce. By the mid-1970s, they had even become cheap enough to be used in simple electronic toys and games. The first microprocessor was made in 1971. This allowed compact computers to be built and paved the way for the explosion in computer and video games.

PADDLE GAMES
The first video game sold was called Pong because it was similar to electronic table tennis, or Ping-Pong®. It had simple graphics and controls.

— television

— console

— hand controllers

CONSOLES
The Sony PlayStation is a state-of-the-art home game console. It is almost as powerful as the game machines found in public arcades.

SCREENS

The Sony PlayStation is used with the latest wide-screen television sets, which originated in Japan.

LAP TIME

1/4

5

km/h

JOYPAD

Each player uses a handheld control, called a joypad, to control the game.

OPEN

PlayStation

SELECT START

DESIGN A HANDHELD GAME

You can't make a real computer game, but you can have fun designing one. Make some sketches of your game console. It needs a screen, four direction buttons, and some fire buttons.

TOY SYNTHESIZERS

There have always been toys that are simple versions of things in the grown-up world. Today, children can play with toy synthesizers that actually make music electronically. Some of them have memories and can play back, as well as supply background music. Instruments available include keyboards, guitars, drumsets, and saxophones. Many have microphones for singing along, sometimes incorporated in an electronic headset.

microphone headset

guitar synthesizer with built-in recording tape

VIDEO GAMES

A video game console is a specialized computer that can draw graphics very quickly on a screen. It is programmed to play different games when different electronic cartridges or compact discs are loaded into it. Instead of a keyboard, the console has a joystick or keypad. You control the game by moving the joystick or pressing the buttons on the keypad. Many video games involve battling with aliens on another planet, fighting the forces of evil in a fantasy land, or finding your way through a series of puzzles or obstacles. During the game, the computer constantly checks your input and figures out how this affects what happens to the characters or places in the game. It uses this information to construct the relevant picture on the screen.

The screen of a handheld game is actually made up of a grid of thousands of tiny squares. The electronics in the console send a tiny electric current to the squares it needs to darken to make a picture.

ADVANCES IN ELECTRONIC TOYS

Since the first simple electronic devices were made in the 1950s, they have quickly become more and more complex. The toys that use electronics have become more complex, too.

1970s
A simple electronic game. The players must remember the order in which the colored lights flash, and repeat it by pressing the buttons.

VIRTUAL REALITY

Virtual reality is a make-believe world, created by computer, designed to make you think it is real. All the details of the make-believe world are stored in the computer's memory. The world might be a fantasy land, the inside of an ancient building, or life on another planet. From the stored details, the computer builds a picture of what the world looks like from any point of view. Wherever you look in the pretend world, the computer draws what you would see. You are fooled into thinking that you really are in the pretend world, because the picture is shown in a headset that makes it appear three-dimensional. You press buttons on a joypad to move around in the make-believe world.

1970s
The Stylophone, a British toy, is a battery-powered, handheld electronic organ. You play the keyboard with a special electronic pen.

1980s
Electronic chess games are small computers programmed just to play chess. They can play at several different levels — from beginner to Grand Master.

1990s
Handheld video consoles contain powerful electronics that create moving pictures on the color screen.

Inside a virtual reality headset, there are two screens, one for each eye. Each screen shows the world from a slightly different angle. The two pictures come together in your brain to make you see one, three-dimensional, picture. When you move your head to look around, the headset detects the movement and alters the picture accordingly.

GLOSSARY

ARCHAEOLOGIST A person who studies the past by looking at ancient objects, ruins, and literature.

AXLE A rod around which a wheel turns. Axles are used in cars, trains, and other vehicles.

CERAMICS Another word for pottery or anything made of clay.

CLOCKWORK A mechanical device that uses the energy released by a powerful spring to make a clock or toy work.

COMPONENT One part of a whole object.

COMPOSITION An artificial material developed for molding dolls' body parts.

CONSOLE A control panel used for operating computer games.

COUNTERWEIGHT A weight that keeps a toy from toppling over. It forces it upright if it begins to fall too far to one side.

ELECTRONIC Something that is operated by an electrical circuit. It is made up of small components, such as transistors and capacitors.

FLAMMABLE Any material that would quickly and easily burst into flames if you set it on fire.

FLATS Model soldiers or other figures made from flat pieces of metal. They have molded shapes on one or both sides.

FLYWHEEL A heavy wheel that stores energy used to power a toy. You will find flywheels in toys such as model cars.

GRAPHICS Drawings or designs produced by hand or by computer. Computer graphics are widely used in computer games.

GYROSCOPE A device that resists movement. Inside a gyroscope is a very fast-spinning flywheel.

HOBBYHORSE A toy horse consisting of a horse's head on the end of a pole. You sit astride the pole to ride the horse.

MECHANICAL Something that is operated by a system of cogs or wheels and levers, rather than by electricity or other means.

MOLTEN METAL A liquid made when a metal is heated so much that it melts.

OPTICAL Anything to do with light and how you see light.

PAPIER-MÂCHÉ Papier-mâché (literally, mashed paper) is made by soaking strips of paper in water and paste. When it dries, the soaked paper forms a hard material.

PHONOGRAPH A device that records and plays back sound. The phonograph was the first recording machine. It preceded the record player.

PORCELAIN Very fine, delicate china pottery.

PROTOTYPE The prototype of an object is a working version of the object, built to scale. It is used to check whether or not the final object will work properly.

SPINDLE A very thin rod, often used to twist or wind thread.

SYNTHESIZER An electronic musical apparatus that can reproduce the sounds of several traditional instruments.

SYNTHETIC Artificial, or man-made.

THREE-DIMENSIONAL Something that has height, depth, and breadth; that is, something that looks true to life.

VACUUM MOLDING A process used to mold plastic sheets into different shapes by sucking them onto a mold while they are soft.

INDEX